HOW SOCIAL MEDIA CHANGE OUR LIVES

….Social Media is Changing the Way We Live Our Lives

By

WALEED ALAWADHi

LEGAL DISCLAIMER

The Author and Publisher has strived to be as accurate and complete as possible in the creation of this book, notwithstanding the fact that he does not warrant or represent at any time that the contents within are accurate due to the rapidly changing nature of the Internet.

While all attempts have been made to verify information provided in this publication, the Author and Publisher assumes no responsibility for errors, omissions, or contrary interpretation of the subject matter herein.

Any perceived slights of specific persons, peoples, or organizations are unintentional. In some books out there, like anything else in life, there are no guarantees of results.

Readers are cautioned to rely on their own judgment about their individual circumstances and act accordingly. This book is not built for use as a source of legal, medical, business, accounting or financial advice. All readers are advised to seek services of competent professionals in the legal, medical, business, accounting, and finance fields.

TABLE OF CONTENTS

INTRODUCTION

Hello,

Thank you for downloading this amazing guide — **"HOW SOCIAL MEDIA CHANGE OUR LIVES: Social Media is Changing the Way We Live Our Lives."**

If you haven't noticed, there is a revolution taking place in the online world. Well, there are many revolutions taking places these days due to technology, but I am referring specifically to the phenomenon known as "social networking".

According to Wikipedia, Facebook has 2.27 billion active subscribers worldwide. By comparison, the United States population is just above 300 million people, so you could say that Facebook has roughly 7 times of the entire US population. That's a big country.

Of course, the Facebook community is made up of many people from around the world, not just the US. And it's not limited to the under 30 crowds either. While it may once have been right that social networking was a fad in college dorm rooms, today it is a legitimate way of keeping in contact with one another.

Many have joined so that they can share their lives with family and friends who are scattered across the country or around the world.

Social networking, or social media, has completely changed our lives in a short period, and there is no going back. It's like flip this house on steroids, and only, instead of a house, it's you and me.

You could say that most of the change has happened slowly over the past decade. But it's just getting started. I liken social networking to the Truman Show, except we are all both participants and audience members.

We are in the middle of a turning point in the story of humanity. Humanity is becoming a story of its own, one feed, wall post, and tweet at a time. Not all generations have the opportunity to play witness to such pivotal moments in history. You can for one, consider yourself lucky to be a part of it, even if it is 140 characters at a time. *Let's Get Started!*

SOCIAL MEDIA AND OUR LIVES

The different forms of social media available today have in no little way affected the cause of human existence. As various types of media continue to spring up in addition to television, the print media, radio and the internet, so many lives are being influenced either positively or negatively.

Social media as experts have been able to decipher considerable effect on both young and old. The famous saying that we are products of what we read, watch and hear cannot be overemphasised.

A good number of children have been found to derive some of their appropriate behaviour or specific pattern of expression as a result of movies which they've watched. Children can take on very remarkable traits from what they've seen on social media such as TV or what they heard on the radio.

A good example is a young child who disturbs the parents to get him attire like the one the surgeon had on him for a TV advert. The toddler may even mimic the way the surgeon speaks. And of course, this can go a long way to arouse the curiosity and the genius embedded in that little one.

Adults are not left out of this too. However, on the other hand, a lot of vices in society have erupted today as a result of some of the scenes, even advertorials being featured on some of the social media. In fact, in very many cases some of the adverts and appearances on the TV and a good number of websites are targeted at arousing sexual feelings.

Truthfully, quite a number are even dedicated to pornographic images. And of course, these can go a long way to affect the psyche of anyone that stumbles on such corrupt social media practices for a lifetime, either old or young. Most cases of rape are as a result of some the appearances on the media.

How about violence too? Again, one of the ills of the media which has culminated into evil in the larger society is the issue of violence being featured on the mass media. As good as the social media is, it has also been to the detriment of a lot of people around the globe.

Well, quite a lot is being done to put a check on social media ills. We now have Parental control features on some devices, and many countries also have regulatory bodies which have been empowered to put a check on some forms of social media. But in this crucial issue, it is not the checks by the regulatory bodies or the parental control that matters.

We must clamour for a society which is healthy and void of vices. So are we willing to change as an individual? Or are we ready to go the extra mile to give children the opportunity to grow up in an environment void of the negative extremes which social media may at times bring? The choice is ours.

Social networking

Social networking is not just for friends and family either. LinkedIn provides a unique online setting for working professionals to broadcast their resumes to the world. They can also use LinkedIn to join industry trade groups, network with other like-minded individuals on business ideas, and search for jobs.

Recruiters and employers use LinkedIn to find new, qualified applicants, many times without paying a fee (although there is a fee-based service for employers who want to post classifieds and have easier access to the many potential candidates on the site).

Spigit offers companies the ability to have their own internal social networking websites, where employees can collaborate on new ideas and innovations in real time without having to be in the same place, all the while keeping the information shared private and confidential to the company.

Even the FBI and CIA have jumped on the bandwagon. They are implementing their top secret version of Facebook. According to the assistant deputy director of national intelligence, "it's every bit Facebook and YouTube for spies, but it's much, much, more".

Next, we have YouTube or television for tomorrow. With YouTube, you can become a superstar almost overnight, so long as you have a video camera and access to the internet. For example, there is the famous YouTube sensation, Fred, a 15-year-old child actor with over 1 million subscribers. Many of his videos have over 2 million hits, some of them upwards of 5 million hits, and he even has his line of t-shirts through a sponsorship deal with Hot Topic.

Next, we have Susan Boyle, the worldwide phenomenon from Britain's Got Talent. Susan has earned her place in the internet history books quietly because she sang one song that made the world smile.

Without YouTube, she'd more than likely be a small-time sensation in the UK rather than the global household name she is now. Her first performance of the famous "I Dreamed a Dream" from the Broadway hit Les Miserable has been viewed more than 150 million times on YouTube.

Then there is Twitter. A place where a college student can correspond with his congressman about an upcoming bill; a 12-year-old can follow the minute-by-minute details of her favourite celebrity, down to what she is having for dinner; and some geek in Idaho can "tweet" with some geek in India about the next great video game.

Of course, to regulate our disdain for information overload, Twitter requires that all communication be done in 140 characters or less. So it may not be the best platform for the long-winded among us.

What's great about Twitter is that it is sort of like a microblog or a Facebook status update that you keep updating as much as you want. You can also use it to connect with anyone without them permitting you to follow their updates (although there are privacy controls, many people on Twitter opt out of them).

It means that any person can follow any celebrity, politician, or regular ole Joe so long as they have their Twitter name. Ashton Kutcher recently beat CNN in a contest to see who could reach 1 million Twitter followers first. Aston won. But the neat thing is that many celebrities and notable figures not only use it as a platform to voice their own opinions, they actively tweet back with many of their followers regularly.

It could not be done before Twitter. If anything, Twitter has become the great equaliser in how we communicate and share information. You don't have to be a movie star or political figure to make your voice known. And many people are using it today to earn their mini celebrity status (some of them with thousands of followers of their own).

THE WISDOM OF CROWDS

We cannot help but face how radically our lives have been changed on a daily basis by social media. Let's face it, we've all become social media junkies, and it has both positive and negative effects, but it is undeniably influential.

We now can instantly share our thoughts, create social gatherings, and receive updates on major world events as they happen. We are connected in a way that was never before possible, and it's easy to take it for granted.

Our Personal Lives

Back in 2012, there is hardly an aspect of your life that is unaffected by social media. How many of you wake up, get your mobile device and check your Facebook as I do?. What did you find of interest? How did that affect your next decision for the morning? You may have read a post that angered you or made you laugh, but the chances are that left an impression on you as you went about your morning routine. It may have sparked a discussion with your spouse or roommate. Did you receive an invite? Did that help you formulate your plan for the day?
Instead of closing us off from one another, it is bringing us together and enhances how we organise real-time social gatherings and it facilities real-world intimacy rather than shutting it down, as was feared when the media was in its infancy. Humanity has an insatiable desire to find out what's happening out there in the world and Facebook feeds into that as does twitter and even Google Plus, for the few pioneers forging ahead with that social platform. In this way, we can keep up with all of the doings in our friend's lives they choose to post on the net.

The Business World

The biggest boon has been for business. Why? Because market analysts have entire teams devoted to researching trends on Facebook and how we interact with each other. What are the Millennials talking about right now? What are their likes? What are their purchasing habits online and what do they say about your company and your competitors? All of it is valuable as it gives corporations an intimate view of you and how to sell you the products you need and want.

Companies look at your peer group and how they influence your purchasing decisions. They know what products sell to different political ideologies and refine campaign messaging to what interests them and appeals to their emotions. What are the marketing trends of this religion or that and how do we sell to them? What are teenagers passionate about and how can we tap into that? Facebook is the one place where everybody is, and out of 2.27 billion users, they have a lot of data to analyse. Small businesses have a tremendous opportunity now to engage you directly with strategic marketing campaigns for very little investment.

A local business has a better chance now that they can create a Fan Page and interact with you directly.

People tend to buy from who they know and if they see you are a local business and are actively engaging them and finding out what the response to they will go to you over the major corporations, given a choice. It means direct marketing and content marketing is far more active now than it ever has been before.

Our Community

There is no doubt that Social Media has completely transformed how we think of community. Just as in our personal lives, our communities are connected in ways that are still unravelling due to sites like Facebook, Twitter, and Meetup. In 2011, the entire world was changed by The Arab Spring and The Occupy Wall Street Movements. Regardless of your opinion of these events, you cannot deny the role that social media played in these movements. We can now organise events, share our collective experiences, and feel connected to the global community. We are connected and interconnected with hundreds of millions of people at any given moment, thanks to social media. It plays heavily on what humans do best: to join.

This ability produces a deep cross-fertilisation of culture, ideas, thoughts and opinions. This same ability has not only taken the world by storm but changed it as well. With social media, people have become more aware of their surroundings, of situations all over the world. It ignited conversations that eventually led to digital revolutions. Social media has been instrumental in creating cohesion between disparate groups in the Middle East. Twitter and Facebook pushed for popular uprisings of people against their dictatorial governments in Egypt, Syria, Libya and Tunisia. The nature of medium by which the messages were propagated primarily contributed to the speed at which these revolutions and uprisings unravelled.

One nation

The sentiments of one nation virally spread across other regions and sparked not just curiosity, but snowballed emotions as well. People from different continents amplified the calls from troubled nations and pushed their leaders to act. Indeed, it brought about courage from people within; after all, they have the whole world backing them up. The New York Times suggested that social media websites such as Facebook and Twitter helped people organise the political revolutions in Egypt where it helped certain classes of protesters organise protests, communicate grievances, and disseminate information. Social media also allowed for businesses and companies to be more responsive to their customers. Companies have taken the 'wisdom of the crowds' to their advantages, soliciting discussions and debates across much social media platforms as they are could-eventually marketing their products virtually costless, while getting new ideas on how to make their products more efficient and practical at the same time.

Marketers now have the challenge of marketing on a very personal level with potential customers. One good or bad tweet of a consumer can lead to a rippling effect.

Overall, the actual impact of social media lies in one word: change. It is helping the world spark shift in one way or another. It is supporting the world gradually develop in a more humane digital world. It allows for a deeper connection, outside of small texts exchanged from halfway across the world-it brings with its emotion.

Businesses will grow to more customer-oriented companies, rather than profit-oriented. The ability to harness this newfound power lies ultimately to the people who stand benefitted from it.

IMPORTANCE OF SOCIAL MEDIA NOW AND FOR THE FUTURE

Current trends have shown that people now recognise how valuable social media marketing has become. More than anything else this platform for networking has had a significant impact on our day to day life.

If we look back ten or so years, we can take stock of how our lives have changed so much. Tools like Facebook and Twitter were nonexistent ten years ago, but now thanks to advances in technology and the internet, these social communication tools have remarkably changed our lives and how we now communicate and interact with others around the world.

Social media networking has also impacted the way we spend our free time in our daily life. Social networking is not here just for today but also for every day and the future far ahead as it is fast becoming the media for the future.

More and more people young and old are moving away from traditional methods of communicating and this in itself is creating challenges for companies as they now no longer need to spend vast amounts of money on conventional digital media marketing and advertising.

However, you can't pretend this form of marketing is a smooth ride; it takes a lot of hard work. The internet makes this more comfortable as you can track what is happening and maintain all your information with a few keystrokes on a keyboard and clicks of a mouse.

This form of digital marketing can be combined with traditional campaign strategies including direct-response and branding. Today more and more organisations are now using social networks for business purposes including sites like Twitter, Facebook and LinkedIn. Approximately six out of ten companies use social marketing to build and promote their brands and business, improve their communication as well as engage with their consumers.

So, what does the future hold for social media marketing? Well, the most significant change in social marketing will have more and more companies will be incorporating social media directly onto business websites. More and more SEO consultants are providing businesses with packages for integrating social networking as part of their advertising campaigns. For example, many businesses using Facebook to create business pages have seen increased growth. It has led to more and more enterprises buying ad space on Facebook as soon as they begin marketing their business or website. This is a trend that will continue to grow and will eventually encompass all the major social media sites.

The way businesses use social media will also change. Currently, the trend of businesses is to increase their online presence and to do this they are turning to social media sites.

What we need to know

More and more companies will begin to heavily rely on Twitter to inform people of changes, sales and other relevant information. The reality of this is by creating immediate, portable, transferable, on-demand knowledge sources; companies will be able to reach their audiences on a much grander scale than they could ever possibly imagine.

Here is what we do know about social media:

1. Our young people are connected. Today's youth understands social media; they live and breathe it every day. They use the tools as ways to share with their friends.

As kids, we used the telephone. Today's kids use cell phones and MySpace. When you put the cell phone with MySpace, you get Twitter. To any young person, the power of Twitter is a no-brainer.

2. Social media brings on two-way communication. Where email was one-way communication that was often not instantaneous, Twitter is two-way and instant. Furthermore, with Twitter, you can have instant two-way communication with virtually thousands of people at once.
3. Social media enables people to deepen connections and relationships.
4. Social media is here to stay. The way we are communicating is in a revolutionary change and that change centres on social media. Traditional advertising and broadcast media must adapt to this new step-child. Evan Williams, the co-founder of Twitter, said, "Journalists who embrace the new media will thrive; those that don't want."
5. Social media is forcing changes in marketing and sales. The way we discover, evaluate and purchase products and services is experiencing a major insurgency. Word of mouth purchases come not from the neighbourhood pharmacist but from what our friends tell us on Facebook or what we hear on Twitter.
6. Ashton Kutcher taught us that the way we hear about news and events is also changing through social media. The fact that CNN wants 1 million followers tells that a significant network recognises the power of a social networking tool like Twitter.
What are the things we do not know about social media?

1. Where is social media taking us? Where will we be in 5 years? No one has a clue.

2. Which media tools will survive? Is Twitter a fad? Will the little bird be eaten by the big cat, Google? MySpace is already on the decline. What about Facebook? My hunch is that each of these tools will find the right niche. MySpace will survive for the very young. Twitter in some form will survive for instant message type communication world-wide.

3. How will social media affect advertising, public relations, marketing, and sales? I guess that broadcast, intrusive advertising as we know it today, will not survive.

For some products (not many) it will continue in some form. Social media adds a new component to the "marketing" mix. By doing so, traditional marketing efforts must adapt. Time will show us how and who will survive.

4. What's next? We now have Web 2.0 which means an interactive Web. It's much more engaging to read a blog in which you can comment than to read a static website. For that reason, blogs have soared in popularity. What will Web 3.0 or 2.5 or whatever looks like? There are some guru's out there who can share what they see in their crystal balls. But, for most of us, it remains a mystery. The challenge is to be ready. Two things we can count on: we are on the cusp, and there's more to come.

HARMS OF SOCIAL MEDIA

We Need To See The Potential Harm Of Social Media

Before 1794, farms across the world could only pick cotton as fast as humanly possible. In the late 18th century, Eli Whitney discovered the cotton gin and a simple process done since 500 AD was instantly improved upon. This invention took 1200 years and a lot of hard labour before it was discovered. Once this invention was created, it caused efficiencies but also caused concern for a decreased need for labour.

Nowadays we are on a logarithmic scale of technological advancement, leaving us with much less time to evaluate the benefits and risks of new products. As new inventions are created, they are often able to be used instantly without fully understanding the downside.

Social media is an arena that is expanding daily and allowing immediate communication like we have not experienced before. There are a lot of benefits to social media, and the adoption rates are unprecedented. Information is capable of being instantly disseminated, allowing businesses and individuals to be more informed and efficient. This new media has also let friends and family stay connected and for new ideas to be formed.

Social media has positively impacted our society; however, there is a worrying sign about our tendency not to focus on the harms social media may bring.

Addiction to instant feedback

One of the most significant segments of our population that regularly use social media is our children. As a child develops their personality, they are making decisions about how they will react to every situation. As they progress through school, they will make decisions and actions that affect the way they are perceived.

With social media, the feedback is instant, and after posting a picture or a simple statement, they can receive gratitude and excitement from messages that are sent to them following the post.

It can create such a positive response that often leaves a child with an increased urge to do it again. If the video or picture that was posted generated a great response, they often want to find something more spectacular the next time they post.

A desire for acceptance and popularity has existed since the beginning of time, though, now with the ability to communicate with friends for 24 hours a day, the scene is changing. The ability to update a status or post a picture from a phone allows kids to react without thinking instantly. Usually, these actions are benign, but can at times cause irreversible harm.

Recently, social media has been in the press relating to adolescents who got hospitalised after being dared on social media. As a child growing up, many kids will dare others or try something because their friends challenge them. Online, you can become infamous throughout the world instantly, and this has a draw for many kids. Just recently a child was hospitalised after putting a bottle rocket in his pants, and others were hospitalised after holding cinnamon in their mouth for a minute. The danger is that these kids may or may not know that these stunts are dangerous. It may not be evident that a video seen online is not a credible source

Bullying online

Cyberbullying is another dangerous product of social media. The internet is the new playground that our children live in, and it is an unregulated often unsupervised place. Most parents would not let their children play in a park that they have not visited, though, many of us are not aware of what our children are doing online.

As mentioned above, social media can be a place where children can find acceptance and popularity. It also can be a place that is feared and causes psychological harm. If most children are using social media and another child who tries is left out, this could cause that child to feel alone.

On a more extreme level, what might have been contained at school now may be non-stop 24 hours a day. Many instances have resulted in fatal outcomes that were caused by cyberbullying. Most recently, a college kid from Rutgers committed suicide after parts of his social life were exposed on social media. It is becoming a more significant problem, and we need to be more aware of it.

We should be aware of bullying and open to discussing it with our community and children.

Communication

We are being accustomed to quick messages and shorthand typing that we will soon become a society of less social individuals and poor communication skills.

As we move forward, it is imperative that we understand there are many benefits to social media, but also acknowledges the downside. Besides, it is prudent for us to gather as a family, community and a country to sort out the role social media has in our lives.

Our children need us to discuss that there are more things important than achieving notoriety and also that we are there if they need us. It may be difficult to eliminate a dangerous dare or cyberbullying, but we should do our best to minimise the damage and help our children become adults without harm.

The Machine Maketh The Man

With so many social networks flushing us with information all the time, people are leading far more fragmented lives. It's a noise of incomprehensible shouting online as all this information spews out from different streams.

Having the information highway at your fingertips is all very well but what you are contributing isn't promised it would dissolve and permeate its destination. All the information gets lost in the sharing storm and loses its value.

The whole practice becomes a waste of time, and the communication can often be lost. Communicating becomes difficult when it seems like it should be more comfortable.

Sharing becomes something you need to plan to ensure that the message is received on the other side. This obstacle in itself leads to even more sharing as you try to get out onto as many social networks as possible to cover all your bases and this is especially so if you are a brand.

What Etiquette?

People have become worryingly obsessed with social media. iPhones, iPads, Blackberries and Androids dominate more conversations at social gatherings that is acceptable. First of all, it is incredibly bad manners to spend real-life social time Tweeting and to check Facebook on your phone the whole time.

It also isolates you and stops you from interacting with people in a way that would naturally have occurred had social media never existed. People no longer make acquaintance with their fellow man because they use any time they have to isolate themselves exclusively to their mobile phone.

Clearly, it shows people have a lack of self-control or that some rules and etiquette standards need to be put into place to guide them away from the terrible habit of preferring social media interaction to real interaction.

We've allowed ourselves to become less human by limiting so much of our interaction with social media. We by default have become machines ourselves in how we communicate through digital media. Search, and share has also changed the way we think. We've adapted our brains to the likes of Google and other search engines. The cognition change means that in the Age Of Information, we are finding it more and more difficult to recall information.

Strangely we have become better at knowing where to retrieve that information from. The constant easy access to whatever information we want means our brain merely has to focus on where to find it when we need it rather than being able to recall the report itself. Distracted and distorted is this fragmented world of social media may have chosen to live in as avatars. A reality that should be realised is that communication although it may be, social media is not reality. Choosing to live outside of the real world and in cyberspace is a sad step to take when limiting your life to the power of social media.

CONCLUSION

Our world has transformed into a Global Village, connected at all times by the social web. So much is the impact of social in our lives that staying away from it can take you to extinction, and who wants to go obsolete in today's world of fast connectivity?

Remember those times when you hesitated to share your opinion? Today, the social sphere encompasses untrammelled communication devoid of interaction barriers. It enables like-minded individuals to come together and opine on a common platform. It helps in uniting people working for common goals and also gives them a viable direction for investing their efforts.

Don't you wonder how social media has changed us and empowered us furthermore? There is mass empowerment, resulted by the sharing of ideas on the social sphere. Masses have become more empowered and are more informed. It enables individuals to get first-hand information, and the world is becoming a smaller place to live in. There is so much data on the social sphere that it could be very challenging to sift through authentic information. Authenticity is left best to the discretion of the general public, which makes them highly opinionated too. This lack of authoritative information makes most people misinformed and even sparks unnecessary tirades.

Whenever faced with the question of how social media has changed us, one word that comes to my mind is insecurity... Due to the humongous amount of educational exchanges on the social sphere, it has become a leading champion of distrust. It has become one of those channels of communication, which is increasingly being deemed as insecure and untrustworthy. It enables the dissemination of information to untrustworthy audiences, leading to higher crime rates.

It is imperative to exercise caution while using it, but the benefits of social media are too good to be ignored.

Thank You Once Again For Downloading This Fantastic Guide!